Supermum

Mick Manning and Brita Granström

W

FRANKLIN WATTS

065011 NEW YORK • LONDON • SYDNEY

Supermum is everywhere!
Swinging, swooping, swimming, scooting.

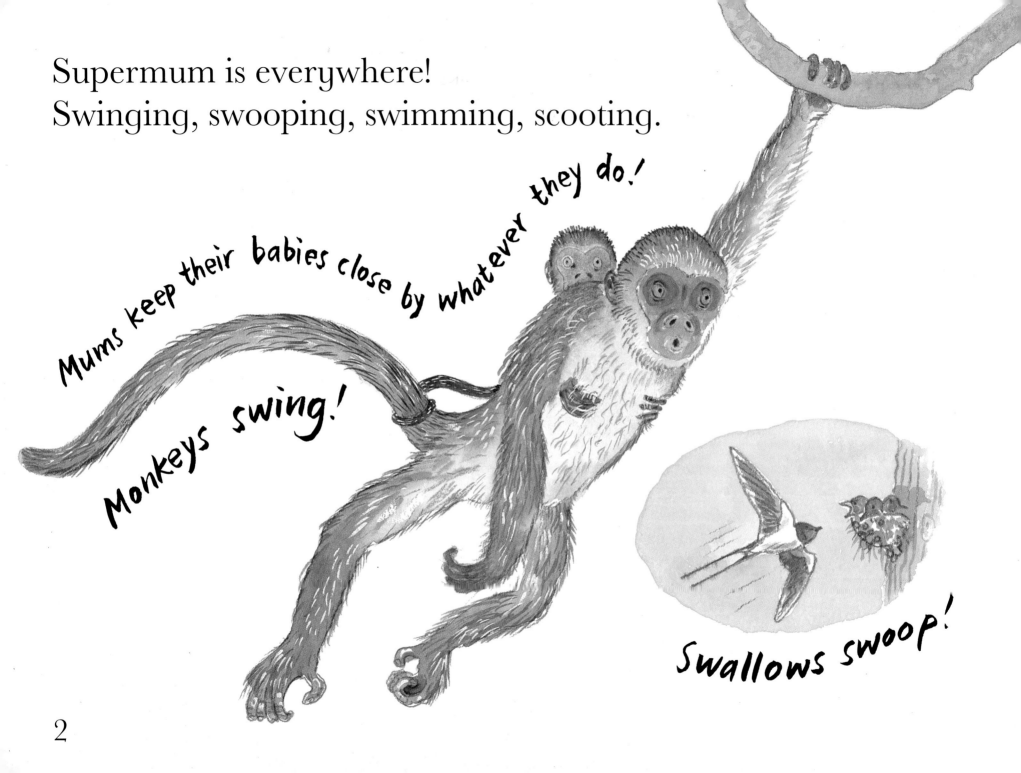

Mums keep their babies close by whatever they do!

Monkeys swing!

Swallows swoop!

2

Supermum comes in all shapes
and sizes, with lots of legs,
lots of fur, a tail, or even scales!

Mouth brooders shelter their
babies in their mouth!

We call the person we grow inside 'mum'. We can call the grown up who looks after us 'mum' too.

Wildebeeste mums have horns.

Shieldbugs make good mums.

5

Supermum has babies!
She lays eggs – or she carries
her babies inside her body
until they're born.

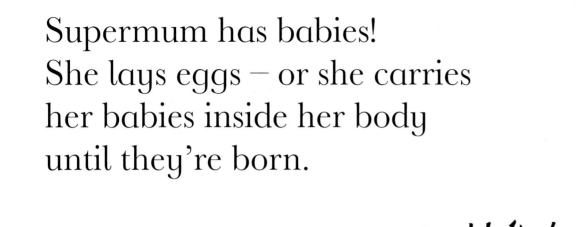

Some snake mums
guard their eggs...

We all need a mum or we couldn't be born.
Mums bring new life into the world.

Blue whales are the biggest mums on earth!

Cats can have lots of babies.

Human mums carry their babies inside their tummy for nine months.

7

Supermum knows the best games –
hide and seek, tickle, king of the castle
and lots of others.

Stoat mums get up to
all sorts of tricks!

Many babies, from wolf cubs to you,
learn by playing with their mum.

Supermum talks to her babies –
in lots of different ways!

11

Supermum will do anything for her little ones!
She'll go out in a storm to get her baby food.

Penguins walk for days to find fish for their babies.
Your mum goes out in all weathers for your food too!

13

Supermum is brave! If you threaten her babies, she'll scratch! She'll fight! She'll bark! She'll bite!

From swans to insects, many mums will fight to protect their babies.

14

15

Tyrannosaurus rex made a good mum. She probably carried her babies in her mouth.

There have always been mums ever since life began, long, long, long ago!

Supermum is gentle!
She might look scary, but she always treats
her own babies **very** carefully.

Mums are very gentle
with their own children.

Supermum knows best!
She knows just what her baby likes to eat.
Worms, beetles or biscuits?
Supermum even knows your favourites.

Different baby animals like different baby foods — and mums know best!

Waspgrubs eat caterpillars. Osprey chicks eat fish...
What do you like best?

Supermum gives the best wash and brush up! She keeps her babies clean and tidy.

Babies need to be clean. Stale food is a breeding ground for germs!

20

Supermum is a nest-builder, a burrower,
a cave-dweller – a home-maker!
She tucks her babies in all sorts of cosy places.

A chimney pot!

A bird's nest!

A hole in
the ground!

Even a crack in a wall ... or a little wooden bed!

Supermum is a cuddle expert!
She'll nurse her babies to sleep, holding them
close while they have the happiest dreams.

Cuddling is a good way for mum and baby to show how much they love each other.

Supermum is wide awake!
Even on the darkest night, she's always
ready to feed her hungry babies.

owl mums hunt mice
in the dark...

Human babies can
wake up anytime
for a feed!

27

Supermum has always been different shapes and sizes…

and she always will be.

Supermum Index

Ant – See page 23. An ant's nest is started by a queen ant. She lays all the eggs that hatch into the thousands of ants that will live there.

Barn owl – See page 26. Barn owl mums hunt for rats and mice to feed to their babies.

Blue whale – See page 6. Blue whale mums have a baby every two or three years.

Brown bear – See page 5. Brown bear mums look after their cubs for over three years.

Cat – See page 7. Cat mums can have a 'litter' of kittens once a year.

Dolphin – See pages 10 and 11. Dolphin mums look after their babies for about a year and a half.

Lynx – See page 25. Lynx mums have between one and five kittens at a time.

Monkey – See page 2. Monkeys carry their babies on their back or around their tummy.

Mouse – See page 22. Mouse mums can nest under floorboards or even in old birds' nests.

Mouth brooder – See page 4. These fish protect their babies inside their mouths.

Orca – See page 3. (Sometimes called killer whales.) Orca mums teach their babies to hunt.

Ostrich – See pages 10 and 11. Ostrich mums lay about 15 eggs at one time.

Penguin – See page 12. Emperor penguins nest in huge colonies a long walk from the sea.

Polar bear – See pages 10 and 11. Polar bears usually have two cubs at a time.

Rabbit – See page 22. Rabbit mums have lots of babies – up to 84 every year!

Raccoon – See page 22. Raccoon mums often bring up their babies in towns and cities.

Shield bug – See page 5. Shield bugs chase away other insects who try to eat their young.

Snake – See page 6. Not all snake mums guard their eggs. Some just lay them and leave them.

Stoat – See page 8. Stoat mums are fierce if their babies are in danger.

Swallow – See page 2. Swallow mums feed their babies squashed-up insects.

Swan – See page 14. Mute swans will attack if you go near their nest. One wing beat could break an arm.

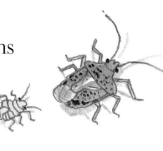

Tiger – See page 20. Tiger mums look after their cubs for two to three years.

Tyrannosaurus rex – See page 16. Tyrannosaurus rex was the largest meat-eating mum that ever existed on land.

Wasp – See page 19. A digger wasp mum digs a small tunnel, lays an egg and leaves a caterpillar for her baby to eat when it hatches.

Wild boar – See pages 10 and 11. (Sometimes called wild pigs.) Wild boar mums have up to ten babies at a time.

Wildebeeste – See page 5. A wildebeeste mum has one baby a year. She always keeps an eye out for danger from lions or hyenas.

Wolf – See page 8. Wolf mums have between three and seven cubs each year.

For our mums – and mums everywhere

This edition 2004
First published in 1999 by Franklin Watts,
96 Leonard Street, London EC2A 4XD

Franklin Watts Australia,
45-51 Huntley Street, Alexandria, NSW 2015

The illustrations in this book were made by Brita and Mick
Find out more about Mick and Brita on www.mickandbrita.com

Series editor: Rachel Cooke
Art director: Robert Walster

Printed in Singapore
A CIP catalogue record is available from the British Library.
Dewey Classification 519.56
ISBN 0 7496 5865 7

BOOKABOO

Dogs In Disguise

This Walker book belongs to:

_____

_____

_____

WALKER BOOKS
AND SUBSIDIARIES
LONDON · BOSTON · SYDNEY · AUCKLAND

It was the Bookaboo Monster Tour.

Bookaboo and the band were on the way to their next gig.

"Tonight we're going to rock my home town," announced Paws. "Paris, here we come!"

"What's Paris like?"
Bookaboo asked the
Cat Nav, turning it on.

Zip! Whirr! Ker-plonk!

Up flashed images of baguettes
and the Eiffel Tower.
But only one thing interested
Bookaboo. "Bookshops,"
he panted excitedly, his tail
twitching. "Let me at 'em!"

"Here we are!" barked Paws excitedly as the Bookabus arrived at the stadium.

But as Bookaboo looked out he saw a crowd of jostling photographers, desperate for a shot of the famous rock band. Bookaboo groaned.

"I can't leave the Bookabus with that lot outside! I'll have to stay here and practise my drum solos instead."

Pow!

Pop!

Just then, a poster outside the window caught his eye.

STORYTIME
at the
Bow Wow Bookshop

TODAY!

"That's what I need," said Bookaboo.

"A story a day or I just can't play! But I'll have to go in disguise."

He started rummaging through all the band's outfits.

Musical instruments, swimming costumes

and dog toys went flying.

It didn't take Bookaboo long to get changed
and no one noticed ten minutes later when he
squeezed out of the window and scampered off.

Certain that nobody would recognize him in his disguise,
he set on his way to the Bow Wow Bookshop.

The bookshop was full when Bookaboo arrived.
He wriggled his way to the front of the crowd.
Nobody had any idea that underneath the wig
was a world-famous rock puppy.

Then a hush fell over the crowd.
Bookaboo felt the familiar tingle in his nose
that always came just before hearing a story.

The Blue Bird

Princess Stories

Dinosaur Days

The General

STORYTIME
at the
Bow Wow Bookshop

The storyteller began. Bookaboo was so excited

he couldn't sit still. He did a quick drum-solo on the floor,

leapt in the air and accidentally knocked off his wig.

Whoops!

The audience turned and stared.

Then they started cheering wildly.

"Bookaboo! It's Bookaboo!"

Meanwhile, in the Bookabus,

Growler was looking for Bookaboo.

He knocked loudly on the bunk.

"Wakey wakey, you dozing doggy," he called.

But Bookaboo wasn't there.

There was just a huge pile of clothes ...

and a poster outside, advertising storytime.

"Oh no!" groaned Growler.

At the Bow Wow Bookshop,

the crowd had gone completely crazy.

Poor Bookaboo.

Luckily, Growler burst in.

"Let's cool down, everyone. Bookaboo needs his story a day

or he just won't play the gig tonight," he said.

It was time to share a story.

The storyteller reached into the Bookabag,
and started to read the story.

When the story was finished, everyone rushed to the stadium for the gig. When Bookaboo led the band onto the stage, the fans clapped and Bookaboo raised his drumsticks.

"I've had my story today and I'm ready to play!"

"LET'S ROCK!"

THE END

First published 2010 by Walker Books Ltd
87 Vauxhall Walk, London SE 11 5HJ

2 4 6 8 10 9 7 5 3 1

Text and illustrations © 2010 Walker Books Ltd
Bookaboo © 2010 Happy Films Limited

Based on the series BOOKABOO developed and produced by Happy Films Ltd

This book has been typeset in Badger

Printed in China

British Library Cataloguing in Publication Data:
a catalogue record for this book is available from the British Library

ISBN 978-1-4063-2654-3

www.walker.co.uk

www.bookaboo.co.uk